Speaking from the autumn of my life

Sarbajit Chowdhury

First Published in October 2019

ISBN: 978-93-5347-830-8

BLUE ROSE PUBLISHERS
www.bluerosepublishers.com
info@bluerosepublishers.com
+91 8882 898 898

Cover Design:
Vandana Kanyal

Typographic Design:
Namrata Saini

Editor:
Apoorva Khare

Distributed by: Blue Rose, Amazon, Flipkart, Shopclues

To my parents and my dearest grandpa, Late Swapan Kumar Gupta, who taught me to live my dreams.

Preface

Poetry is considered to be the "spontaneous overflow of powerful feelings" and it must come as natural as leaves to the trees, as said by Wordsworth and Keats. Poetry must be expressive and these poems contain raw emotions. These poems are a way of looking at the colourful world. These poems deal with the concept of love, lust, freedom, child abuse, marital issues, and several other perspectives. The poems are not to harm any particular individual's sentiments or hurt any believe system. Being an emotional child, I was always expressive but maturity to express my feelings via words came much later and very soon it took the shape of poetry. By god's grace I have been writing poems since a long period of time and I write what I feel and for me poetry is about deep emotional connectivity. And with each passing day my way of expression evolved and reached to a point where I am now. Hope all of you like my work and understand the feelings and deep emotions underneath my chain of words.

Acknowledgement

This was my dream, to give words to my expression and with my due hard work and passion I guess I am able to achieve this feet in my life. First of all, my sincere thanks go to my parents for understanding my passion, my love for poetry. The support I received from my ma and baba is really overwhelming. I would really like to thank my guru ji, Dr Suman Jana, without whose blessings this would not have been possible. Of course, my friends — Ananya, Diti, Subhodeep, and Debarpito —who have been my constant supporters and my motivators to carry on with my dreams. The constant source of positivity and energy was Kavya. Thanks to Dona di for believing in me and making me understand that I can do something big. And of course, I would like to take the opportunity to thank the almighty for such wonderful opportunity. At last but not the least my dear viewers of wandering soul thanks for being so supportive and thanks for showering constant love.

About the Author

Sarbajit chowdhury is a debutant in this world of writing and this book becomes his first book of poems. He lives in the town of Burdwan in West Bengal. He has spent most of his life in Burdwan. He pursued his schooling from St Xavier's School, Burdwan, and completed his graduation from St Xavier's College, Burdwan. He is a born foodie and dwells on junk food. He is a movie buff and a book worm. He loves Hindi and Bengali music. He loves to write and express his view point.

He has an active social media account on Facebook as Sarbojit Chowdhury. He handles a page —Wandering Soul. His Instagram handle is @Iambookworm. The way to contact Sarbajit via email is – sarbogoudec14@gmail.com.

Contents

Divine Beauty

The day was bright with sunny beams,
She walked in with all her gleam,
Draped in her floral dress.
With her flowery fragrance,
Faded away all the stress.
Wrapped with all divinity,
She appeared to be a rare beauty.

My heart was brimming with lust,
My eyes sparkled.
The more I moved close, the more she repelled.
Lust turned to love,
I stole glances of my dear beloved,
And swelled with affection for my little dove.
I struggled to move closer,
Love destroyed her repulsive power.
I pulled her closer,
She looked into my eyes with all love of her.
I could fondle with her hair,
I could feel her flowery aura.
Now she did not repose,
She submitted to my intensity of love,
And let the demon inside me explore.

Those milky white hands caressed deep,
The honey-dipped voice lulled me to sleep.
It was all dark and blank,
But deep down I was happy to have her in my arm.

My slumber was broken by an eternal ray of darkness,
I found myself in a cave full of sadness.
It was well decorated with flowers,
But the way to exit was oblivious.
I searched for the woman divine,
But all in vain.
There was no trace of her,
At last, love was trapped by lust forever.

Lustful Soul

The night was dark and dense,
He strolled down the lane with lustful sense.
His eyes shined with the thought of guilt so adorable,
Guilt he could have avoided,
But indulging was more pleasurable.

The way he touched,
Her soul was bereaved.
She thought, what made her?
Let the wild animal touch her body.
Her soul was lusty,
And the snake bruised her body.
The snake groped the mountains,
And entered the cave,
Where the mundane mystery retains.

The divine treasure was achieved,
And a touch of divinity was received.
The mystery behind the urge of the guilt was realized.
With the rising sun,
A soul was born with the suppressed lust.

Warrior

Success is an illusion,
A road without thorns million.
Adorable to look at,
Harmless to walk,
Impossible to locate.

The cruel world mocked,
"The poor soul," said the world.
Losing his confidence,
He questioned his existence.
Deep down the phoenix,
Was rising, by gathering the broken confidence.
The broken-self stood with all excellence,
He was ready to fight with all vehemence.

The betrayal was unexpectable,
The pain was unbearable.
The experience was enriching,
Adding to his sense maturing.

Happiness is a myth,
Or may be an oblivious truth.
Broken into pieces,
But raising like fallen prince,
With a flame of calmness,
And brightness of experience.
Deep inside the warrior roared,
And gave a final cry,
"Let the war begin!"
This time either do or die.

Savior

She is pure and wild,
Like a blooming bud in a distant forest.
She is unadulterated,
She is blazing,
Like a hearth burning.

She holds impurity, and spreads purity.
Society treats her like filth,
Is she worth the guilt?
She is brave and open,
Not bothered by society so pedantic.
She is forced to be apologetic.
"Men visiting them are unapologetic!
Giving her names, treating her mean,
What about to those men so toxic ?"

Insecurity

It is an engulfing darkness,
Difficult to express,
Hard to endure,
Not giving pleasure,
But still existing.

It chokes, gives you a nauseous,
Head starts paining.
Hand is numb,
And brain turns out to be dumb.
Suffering elementary to go through,
No way to escape through.
Engulfs the happiness
And spreads the never-ending darkness.

A continuous sense of loss,
A feeling so gross,
Making yourself sick.
It's harder to fight,
Harder to feel light,
When it dwells upon you,
Just to crash upon you.

You tend to cling tighter,
But you cannot bring closer.
The loss is inevitable,
Making you palatable,

Making you go down on knees,
Seeking for peace.

Peace is in inner self!
Stronger is the self, who learns to live with,
This engulfing darkness.
And finds happiness,
In this everlasting gloominess.

He

He wanted a companion.
A heart to rely upon,
A person to fall back on,
A soul to love on.

He wanted a soulful connection,
A beautiful relation,
A spiritual amalgamation,
An experience of self-elevation.

He was hungry for love,
Searching for his sweet dove.
A dove on which he can lay his trust upon,
A dove with zero filters on.

He met with parodies of dove.
All veiled with perfection,
All decked up in sweetness,
But his eyes searched for,
An exceptional imperfection.

What he wants? Who wants to know?
Who wants to understand him?
All ready to expect from him,
But none to invest in him.

His Story

He was a failure, allured by mischief,
He chose to act like a thief,
He refused to work hard,
Repelled by success so grand.

The finishing line was near,
To complete the race, he was eager.
Betrayed by luck, he fell on the line,
Shocked by Fate sisters not so kind.

He was criticized by the society,
Exposed to the world's sad reality.
Exiled from his dear family,
He remained snatched of identity.

Life is harsh, ready to crush,
Breaking your self-confidence,
Questioning your efficiency,
Doubting your existence.

Ambition mocked, dreams laughed,
Hopes grinned, and criticism dawned.
He stood against all absurdities,
He fought against all oddities,
Walking all the thorny roads,
He comes back to claim his throne.

Forbidden Road

Thoughts lay inter-twined in his mind,
With dream filled eyes.
He walked the forbidden road,
To achieve something extraordinary,
To live a life he wants, ignoring all taunts,
To walk against the waves of society, so, ordinary.

Societal pressure it was, pulling him backwards,
Distancing him from his passion,
Making him lack emotion.
The conviction paid off,
The dedication mattered all,
And success is what he wanted all.
And people asked, "What is the secret?"
He answered, "To kill the threat."

Friendship

I was breathing gleefully,
I was dreaming cheerfully,
I was in the seventh heaven,
Under thy shape of friendship.

Oh! My friend you were dearer,
Destiny made us asunder,
Or maybe you never liked us happier.
Your one fault,
And here we are filled with enmity,
Once in the coming decade,
I pray for our unity,
Above the façade of right and wrong,
Above the veil of pious and profane,
Under thy shade of friendship.

Love Struck Hard

I loved you in little return,
I expected to be your valentine,
Until the end of time.
I expected to be your companion,
I wanted to be in your heart forever,
I dreamt to be your forever.

But dear destiny, you played foul,
Forever could not even last a decade,
It just took you a couple of seconds,
To break my heat, to crumple my trust.
I have no complain, no question,
But one thing darling, I love you still,
Without any condition.

Rainbowed Love

I chose to love,
Love is said to be red,
But my love is rainbowed.
People question my love,
They say, "You are ill dove."
I am supposed to be outcasted,
I am supposed to be eradicated,
And my love is supposed to be diseased.

What wretched souls are you?
My love is unquestionable as yours are.
My love is daunting,
My love is forever,
Under the proud shadow of rainbowed world.

Darkness

Oh! Darkness, I worship thee,
You give me peace,
You give me ease.
I pledge to be your soul love,
I aspire to be your little dove.
Give me your serenity,
Make me your epitome of purity.

I negate the last streak of light,
Brightness now gives me plight.
I embrace thee my beloved,
And I want to be your sole loved.
Shower me your love darling,
Pull me closer, give me sleep soothing.

Doom You

"Doom you!" cried the lord of guilt,
"You shall be reduced to filth..."
"You moron," cursed the lord of guilt.

The traumatized creature cried,
Fear of failure made him tired.
All seem to crumble down,
All seem to force him down,
To inevitable darkness.

No shelter to rely upon,
No shade as a last savior.
All came crashing down,
Making him cry, "Save me my lord."

In the ambience of darkness,
Came a little of hope of happiness.
A streak of brightness,
A thunder struck the man,
And he was lost in oblivion.

Happy Plight

The air was arduous,
Her eyes were mischievous,
She was a girl with heart magnanimous.
Her hands were like a bunch of flowers,
Her face like a shining diamond,
And her soul was enamored.

Her hair was kept open,
Becoming air's favorite sport.
Every time the hair fell on her face,
She seemed to be a beautiful whirlwind.
She was a beautiful storm with an innocent face,
Whom with all love I will embrace.
That day the journey was full of unknown ease,
She dwelt on her solace,
She rested on my peace.
I felt complete,
No power can deplete, no sorrow can inflict.
We were a whole,
With a divine light,
With a happy plight.
A soul peacefully callous,
Forming a halo beauteous.

Sudden Thrust of Destiny

Life seemed happy and good,
O! I was so jovial and full.
I had plans all set to step on,
I had goals set, to work on.
All seemed so perfect,
All seemed so adept.

All was smile and gleeful,
Then my soul cried, "I am so full."
Laughed the lady of destiny,
Mocked she, "I pity you creature so filthy."
And a sudden thrust I felt,
Oh! I met my fate,
All filled with blood and shadowed by death,
Uttering for forgiveness, "Save me lady from this fate."

That could have been my last breath,
I felt how restful life I had lived.
Never said enough goodbyes,
Never done enough to my genesis,
Never taken enough leaves.
All I could say now let me tell, "I love you."
May be this is our last talk,
May we never hold hands and never walk.
With every inch of my life and love,
Let me say, "I love you, my little dove."

Incompetent Lover's Guilt

It was a dark night,
Spreading its foggy blanket.
We could only hear echo of silence.
O! Lady I applaud your patience.
I was wounded and numbed,
And my sense thrown to oblivion.

You were wrapped like a cute panda,
Unaware of destinies propaganda.
We stared at each other,
We looked into each other's eyes,
And time froze like ice.
All seemed so perfect,
But destiny liked things imperfect.

A few butterflies came in hurry,
Giving me a sense of furry.
I was in sense of awkwardness,
I knew not what to choose for happiness.
We could have walked hand in hand,
Neglecting the demand.
Oh! My Lady I was dumb,
I was incapable of holding your hand.
I was a coward human,
I was a worthless to be a man.

Oh! My lady, I left you full of grieve,
You were kind enough to forgive.
I was ready to be the subject of your wrath.
But you were capable to show me your worth.
I am sorry, my heart's conqueror,
I am your prisoner.
I ask for forgiveness,
I pray for your kindness.

I have one last wish to make,
Do not take my love to be fake.
Judge not the depth of my feeling,
My love! It is ever increasing.
You made me brave enough,
Now I stand holding your hand stout enough.

Again, I was Ready to Love

Dear wind, was again sweet to me,
The moon again appeared beautiful to me,
The stars were again bright to me.
My heart blushed again,
My eyes smiled again,
And filled to the brim,
With gleeful dream.

That was a full moon night,
With bright stars beside.
There was a feeling of rush,
My cheeks were rosy with blush.
The aura was melodious,
The hour was pious.
Heart was again ready to love,
I found my little dove.

Ode to the Eyes

O! You say those to be eyes,
I say that to be beautiful vice.
I see my forever in it,
I see my deep love in it.

It is a replica of your innocence,
It is a proof of your experience,
A happiness surrounded with sadness.
I promise to absorb all your plight,
I wish to make your life full of delight.
Let me be a worshipper of those innocent eyes,
Let me adore where lingers my love,
Let me say, "I love you, my little dove."

Lost Summer Days

The night was windy,
The boisterous brook was bully.
Cloud was fit to roar,
Rain was about to reach the door.
All nature seemed to scream,
To negate the reality as a dream.

Among these, like a bunch of cyclone,
Came a man alone,
With all power and manhood in his sleeves,
With a grin on his lips.
A devilish smile all over his face,
And calmness in his pace.

A lad quite alone in the street,
Struggling his way to flee.
Blinded by the windy rage,
He was devoid of courage.
He felt a sudden touch!
Familiar was the encroach.

Poor lad! Little he knew,
The venom the vile man will spew.
The touch of that hand,
Just ruined the innocence of lad.
He cried for aid,
All turned a deaf ear to the child.
Now a year passed,

The boy lay silent and calm,
No more smile, no more laugh.
The summer was long gone,
Now lies winter lone.

Long Winter Halts

There was a cloud of sadness,
There was shroud of darkness,
There still prevails the winter.
Innocence long torn,
The lad lay forlorn,
An innocent withered,
A sweet flower was smothered.

A dead piece of flesh he was,
Cold and dead it was all,
What was warm, was is scared heart,
A pain that was burning like a hearth.
Still prevails the touch,
Still familiar was the encroach.

Came a voice from within,
All power he gathered to win.
The vile man was ready to spew,
He shouted "No!"
That was the end he needed to go.
The serpent was thrown away,
His wounds were a bit healed away.
"Baby steps," he said to himself,
The long winter withers away.
The ship was ready to prevail,
The ship was about to sail,
To a land that demon cannot avail.

The scars remained all bright,
Still making him puke every night.
Now came the strong self,
Who believed in no story of elf.
His truth was, demon exists,
We need to fight to exist.
A brave man was out at that hour,
Who learned to be strong,
And not to show the chink in the armor.

Wheel of Time

When the night dawns upon,
Sitting by the fire you doze off.
Now, you like the cozy warm fire,
But you are afraid to light the fire.
The warmth of blood is frozen down,
All dreams are thrown off to oblivion.

Let the memory churn you up,
How proud you were?
How your chin was always up.
Always bloated about your beauty,
Always boasted how you fulfilled your duty.
Always proud of your conviction,
Always singing about your dedication.

Now, rolling comes the wheel of time,
Your life is as sour as lime.
You have no more power to move the mountain,
No more butterflies you can retain.
Oh! Man, you get reduced to earth,
Your life used to be a blazing hearth.
Now, all glory gone long ago,
Now, sit and repent your ego.
Man! Now you sit and wait for last call,
And think, "What it takes to end it all?"

Whatever it takes?

What it takes to fulfill your ambition?
It demands your conviction,
It calls for your dedication.
You serve with all purity,
You fulfill all your duty,
With dream full of clarity.

The eyes never forget to dream,
The walk seems as smooth as cream,
You sacrifice your sleep,
You delve deep into utmost depth,
Giving, if possible, your life,
And striving hard to survive.

You think it to be all pleasurable,
You think it all sweet and adorable,
No harm to want a blooming rosy way,
But not easy to accept the thorn that comes the way.
Life loses its all meaning,
All seems to be an illusion,
All complains are beaming,
But you are left into a delusion.
All broken, all lost to extreme,
But it is your wish to achieve the dream.

To, All Merciful

All was cool and calm,
Sleep was still to come,
Thoughts, knocking out my head,
Dreams buried deep down dead.
People all lying in the ocean of serenity.
A lie into the deep ocean of anxiety.

The waves of destiny are unknown,
The shore to be reached is oblivious,
But the dedication is only obvious.
Oh! I am reminded of my deadly sins,
God may be looking upon me with a grin,
"Now face your deed," cried the fate sisters,
The destiny mocked, "Now face your luck, spinster."

O God! I beg for your forgiveness,
O Lord! I plead for your kindness.
All I could say you are all merciful,
For one last time my dear lord,
Make me a lad successful.

I lay all Open and Blank

I lay all open and blank.
My bed lies crumpled,
And I see my world crumbled.
The grey lingers in my mind,
I learn paticncc to be a lesson so kind.

Thoughts get juggled up,
I lay buckled up,
I am brought done by situation,
Leading to my full destruction.

Let the time change eternally,
Let me again breathe freely,
Let me live my dreams completely.
I will build with the broken pieces of my heart,
I will build a world full of peace so great.

To My India

India is heart of emotions,
India is a bunch of cultures,
India is a horde of languages,
India, an amalgamation of happiness!

India a land of love,
Sweet like a little dove.
India a land so diverse,
India is in my heart.

Many expression of happiness,
Many expression of sadness,
Many expression of anger,
But one expression of patriotism.
The happiness we receive,
The freedom we cherish,
Is a boon of your discreet.
Take a bow all freedom fighters,
For whom we have future brighter.

Freedom

Eyes are filled with tears,
With pain in my heart so sheer.
The world is so cruel,
Playing role so dual.
All seems to be a lie,
As all the hope seems to die.

Warrior! What we call?
But we never discuss the fall,
The wounds he bore deep in his heart,
The never healed scars,
That never seemed to be far.
All we discuss is glory so fine,
Ask me the reason, why I pine?
Ask me why I am so kind?
I lay prostate at your feet,
Believing in your vision,
I ask for a way out of guilt,
A narrow ally to the freedom,
Which I prefer rather than this serfdom.

Lost in the busy world

The sun was at its last glory,
The birds were in the utmost hurry.
All the vehicles treading their way,
All human turning their negatives away.
The night is about to spread its pall,
And there lies me negating my heart's call.

The puff of air is smoky,
And full of my agitation.
Mind find its way to ultimate frustration,
And heart finds its way to desperation.
Wishes are blown by a puff of wind,
Perseverance forgotten long as a lesson so kind.

All seems to be devoid of light,
All seems to be ripped of things bright.
Destiny with all its inevitability,
Comes to pounce upon me with utmost ability.
Mind says, "Work hard to achieve great."
Heart says, "For peace take some rest."

To, my lost yellow flowers

In a mind full of thoughts dusky,
Where a prominent voice turns husky,
Lies my conscious full of insecurity.
Where dwells relation so inconsistent,
Lies thoughts of loosing people so consistent.
The greenery of my lively garden fades away,
Taking my yellow flowers away.

The sky is stripped with specks of green,
The surrounding is full of grim,
And I lie on the floor with a grin.
The puff of smoke withers in the air,
My pain deserves no ear,
And I lay forlorn singing my songs of pain so dear.

I lay strangled with absurdities,
Fearsome of oddities.
The relations for which I pine,
Are long lost and not so fine.
Let the rusted chain be loose,
To let go frail bond I choose.
Let the illusions so well wrought,
Be at once unwrought.

To, my beloved

He came in husky steps,
Risking his life, he arrived on her doorstep.
His heart was thumping,
He was arduous,
His eyes were mischievous.

Stood his beloved all decked,
She was an epitome of simplicity,
Magnifying her sanctity.
She was all a bunch of serenity,
She was pure and knew no vanity.

He walked in straight,
All were quiet,
And all seemed so obvious.
Both sat in complete ease,
And urged time to cease.
No wine was sweeter than her eyes,
No rose rosier than her lips.
All seemed to transcend time,
And all in perfect hymn.

A raven as black as puff of darkness,
With all probable gloominess flew in,
And the sad news of departure was brought in.
He was now in hurry,
She was in a sublime furry.
He was ready to take leave,

And she was ready to grieve.
He looked back in her eyes,
She tried to hold back,
As if it was in her rights.

That night they were on the same bed,
No bodily touch could ever raid,
No voluptuous passion was there,
Only swift flowing comfort prevailed there.
The moon was bright in the sky,
The fairies came to spy.
"Blessed them," said the universe.
No malignant could ever cause distress,
The room was full of peace
All seemed to be on perfect ease.
A shrill cry of reality came screeching,
All chains of dream breaching.
Reality dawn upon,
The boy left his heart on pawn
A deeply felt guilt,
If that night he could halt,
All things might have differently felt.
If could the past be mended,
To be with her that night he could have wanted.

My Winter Garden

It was a summer once,
All bright and sunny it was,
My garden was filled with flowers,
All speckled with flowers both red and yellow,
And I loved each of the fellow.
All seemed warm and cozy,
And dearest was the flower rosy.

Summer comes to a halt
Snow was falling and I am ready for the jolt.
The flower starts to wither,
My fellow yellows,
Became very pale and shallow,
My fellow red,
Almost seemed to be dead.

All the yellow withered away,
Smashing my smiles on their way.
I longed for that summer,
But came winter cooler.
I strolled down my snow-filled garden,
The yellows were lost to oblivion,
But in one corner like a wonder,
Survived the red in all wonder.

I moved closer, to be an observer,
I was happy to see the wonder.
The red was blooming amidst the snow,

And a yellow bud was there amidst the snow.
I saw the yellow and red blooming together,
They past the winter and summer,
And they bloomed stronger and merrier.

Oh! Society Beautiful?

A *saree* you do not drape?
O! Then no wonder you are raped.
You smile at the boys?
No wonder they tore you like toys.
The skirt is short of length!
O! It's good that your body is drenched.
You slapped the boy that teased?
O! It's mandatory for you to be ceased.
You are girls! You have to be in limits,
They are boys! They are free of all limits.

Yes, I ask you my society?
She was innocent like a flower with purity,
A beautiful doll, with a sweet smile,
She wore pretty frocks and was covered well!
It was her fault? And not of creature vile?
What provoked the filthy touch?
Oh! I think you did not hear that painful ouch.
I feel no candles to be lit,
But the criminal to be lit.
Let the victim be at ease,
But let the criminal not be at lease.

Let's hear the cry, "Burn them all."
And tear them apart,
So that the soul may rest of the depart,
Let no more star cease from twinkling,
Let them all be eternally sparkling.

My Hero

Hurdles were definitely on my way,
But my concrete believes paved them away.
The sun was shining bright,
But I guess my smile was brighter.
My eyes met his eyes,
And world froze into ice.
My breath stopped,
And stopped my world.

His voice was divine,
And his presence was like wine so fine.
When I reached the man so kind,
My life was full of moments so divine.
His touch was enigmatic,
And his personality was captivating.

O! My hero! You inspire me.
O! My hero! A man so fine,
O! My hero! A man so kind,
Be the star that you are,
May not I reach to you,
But my love will reach to you.

Falling Prey

The sky was lit with moonlight,
And my heart is light too.
What is full of thoughts,
Is my mind,
And my conscious not so kind.
I am buckled down,
And my defense is broken down.

I look up for aid,
But none turn their head.
I suddenly felt something engulfing me,
Spreading its root were complexities,
Spreading its branches were anxieties.
All I could do is bear the creepy feeling,
And let it wound me beyond any healing.

With each passing second the breath becomes heavier,
With every passing minute everything becomes blur,
All seems full of grey,
And falling as a prey.
The thoughts follow as a black cat,
Ready to pounce upon a grey rat.
All I can do is be full of patience,
And let fall all my sense.
All I feel is to wait for the death so calm,
But, alas! He is also not eager to come.

The world so real

The sunlight was all over,
And smiled the sunflower.
The bees were happy,
And the birds were cheery.
All the people being merrier,
And all animals being happier.

They say it to be summer,
I say it is the ideal season of lover.
Happy is the creep,
And happy is thc thief.
All simile is the king,
And all glee is the clown.
All basking in the happy sun,
The thought of being sad and lost in oblivion.

The winds are becoming high,
And higher is their merry spirit.
All were under the illusion,
That sadness is a delusion.
The sun became a bit dim,
And the heart was on the fingertip.
Clouds were covering the sun so bright,
Dull it looked, all colour was lost,
But the confidence was bright.
The believe was strong and,
Self-belief was the strength.

May come all the rain,
May all the colour drain.
All colour may be lost,
Let sadness be the host.
But confidence may never leave,
And strong may be self believe.

In search of ideal flower.

The smile was always present,
And pain was also vehement.
The man meets several flowers,
And meet them for hours.
That is what is called special,
Maybe it keeps him happy eternal.

He laughs loud like a hound,
His voice is a deep sound,
Give a sense of thrill deep down.
He adjusts a colorful veil,
But all his pretense fails.
All he imagines,
Everything will be in place,
In a very slow pace.

He walks down with a happy face,
But sadness slowing down his pace.
He is surrounded with colorful flower,
All saying, "I am best for the hour."
He walks, he talks,
But all he understands is vague.
He still searches that one flower,
That will heal him every second,
Every minute and every hour.

Crimson red

That day all were happy,
And I was the happiest.
My head was crimson red,
And I had my sadness shed.
I was happy to have a life partner,
The one who held my happiness higher,
All seemed eternal and merrier.

A year went by and crimson faded,
And so, my happiness was dead.
My bright face was full of sadness,
Of bruises and of indelible scars.
My crimson red forehead,
Has now proved to be the burial for my dreams dead.

The man of my life and dreams,
Became the reason of my screams.
My expectations were ruined,
And my happy married life buried.
I question my existence,
And the flaws responsible for the situation,
I could only find loyalty,
I could only find trust and love,
As my tremendous flaws.

It became so suffocating, taking my dreams away,
And taking my vibrancy away,
Leaving my bruised smile on the way.

The chains were held tight,
And power was all in its might.
Then came the last cry for self,
Without any longing for help from the elf.
I broke the chains straight,
Washed away the crimson red forehead,
With myth of happy marriage dead.
I stand strong with my identity,
Devoid of any guilt and fright.

O! I forgot to tell you

O! I forgot to tell you,
I had a perfect life,
And yes, I was called the perfect wife.
My husband was happy so was my child,
They were full of glee and with no sadness to hide.
I lived in a huge mansion,
Which was devoid of any invasion.
My husband had a huge car,
But that was definitely not to hide any emotional scar.

O! I forgot to tell you,
I had my closet full of dress,
Both colourful and dull,
But devoid of any stress.
My jewelry box was full of gold,
And I had no grudge to hold.
My husband kept me happy,
And my child kept me happiest.
I had a happy life,
Without any taste of lime.

O! I forgot to tell you,
I loved my child and he loved me,
I loved my husband and he loved me.
I had a life what is called perfect,
With not a tinge of what is called imperfect.
I was in my own happiest world.

O! I forgot to tell you,
I have crossed threescore of my life,
With not a single strife in my life.
My husband has fallen asleep,
Under the ground,
I guess, there sleep is profound.
There once sprung a beautiful flower,
But now remain,
Only the memory of once beautiful flower.
My child lives in a foreign land,
He has a beautiful son,
My only grandson,
I guess I have never met him,
As my memory becomes dim.

O! I forget to tell you,
I still live in a big mansion,
Devoid of any invasion.
I still posses my husband's huge car,
Which was off course not to hide any emotional scar.
I rule the house all alone,
And I had to love the word forlorn.

O! I forgot to tell you,
Now it's time for the tea,
I walked down to the café on the other lane,
Sit there with my only friend,
A stick, with no façade of being feign.
My eyes are stuck on the crowd below,
Where an infectious vibrancy flow.
O! I forgot to tell you,
I am happy and smiling,
Without any wounds for healing?

Winged Dreams

Hopes were soaring high,
All seeming easy,
And hardship seeming a potent lie.
The dreams were getting its wing,
Trying to grab every possible trophy,
And singing the song of win.

The sky seemed the limit,
The situation seemed to be bright,
And every thought was devoid of fright.
Came a voice so divine,
Words were not so fine,
Ordering me to be on ground,
Showing my place to be lowly found.

Young was the age,
With no intention of being a sage,
I choose to be vehemently rebel.
I am not easy to buckle down,
Nor it is easy to break me down.
You can chop my wings,
But you cannot break my will.
I can fight for my dream,
I can break the frame,
To achieve feet higher,
To shatter a frame better.

Broken Heart

Night was dark and silent,
Eyes filled with droplets.
Heart filled with anger
Voice choked with rage.

Tears rolled down, knees bent down,
I screamed, I howled,
And broke the shackles so saddened
Feelings were played with,
My heart was stabbed,
My soul was bereaved,
My power to believe was killed.

You make me clueless,
You render me emotionless,
Still I stand dauntless,
Fighting against all gloominess.

Trying to break free

In the middle of the night,
I hear the silence singing,
My eyes are still blinking,
I try, yes, I try hard,
To stop the thoughts from coming,
The more I bar them, the more they come gushing.

It gives me immense pleasure,
It gives wings to my hidden desire.
I try to mend my thoughts,
Plead them to be rational,
But they are bound to be emotional.
I try to direct their way,
But somehow, they slip away.

Down in my heart I feel hopeless,
I feel it to be complete hollow,
Shaping no concrete thought to follow.
All it does, reminds me of my empty life.
I cry for aid, I scream,
I want it to be a dream.
All I could feel is a heavy burden,
I feel I am tied to a mountain,
The more I try to break free,
The more I am caught in a spree.

My sweet little dove

The night was silent and calm,
The fairies of sleep denied to come.
I lay awake and thoughtful,
About the beauty that is flawless,
About the elegance that is effortless.
I guess, I am in a reverie,
About the sweet and beautiful smile,
About that captivating way of life.

She is full of life and positivity,
Her identity, is her serenity.
She has a heart like ocean,
Her love filled eyes work as a potion.
I am lost in the garden of flowers,
Where grows rose every hour,
Roses all thorn less and smooth,
Just like her voice that sooth.

The bird's soulful voice,
All less attractive to her honey-dipped voice,
Her smooth and black hair,
Is touched with love from the air.
She is a complete beauty,
Filled with complete love,
You are my sweet little dove.

I wait for thee

It never ends, the wait for,
The arrival of thine,
My source of happiness,
And the reason, why I pine.
The hours not talked,
The seconds not spent together,
All reminds me how far you are.

You are like the fresh wind,
Giving solace and peace of mind.
You are like that blooming bud,
Full of hope and beauty unparalleled.
You are calm and pure as dew,
No power can allure you.

The dawn passes into broad daylight,
The noon fades into dusky light,
And at last, comes the night,
With all hidden corrosive plight.
My wait never ends,
My urge to meet you grows stronger,
But, we are destined to lie asunder.

You, my dove,
You are that thorn less rose,
Never to be found,
Never to be brought close,
All I can do, is dream of those hours,
Which will be ours and only ours.

The Messy Dusk

It was a beautiful dusk,
The voices were husk.
The birds were returning,
And the evening was dying in night's arm.
The hour caused no harm,
And all seemed full of charm.

It seemed god blessed the hour,
And rain washed away all the rancor.
The surroundings turned cool,
And the restlessness was let loose,
Giving a sense pleasing,
And all stress ceased,
Giving an easy feeling.

The clouds were messy,
Full of dark and feeling uneasy.
The mind felt liberated,
But somewhere the heart was coveted.
The wishes were long burnt,
And so were dreams long dead,
And reality struck with its strong head.

Trap of Thoughts

I lay in bright sunlit day,
All thoughts plied up like hay.
My heart is dry, my ears not ready to hear,
But my eyes are full of tears.
I am losing the hope and light,
And I feel groped by fright.

I never think of taking a back step,
I am always ready to fight,
But I feel like tied with a tape.
I try to free myself,
Try to speak, to defend my unknown self.
The words get dried up in my mouth,
And giving birth to a mammoth.

I shout and cry,
I howl and become desperate,
To vent out my sadness,
To break the never-ending silence.
I have lost my way to defense,
I see a well stitched trap,
Falling on me and making my life a crap.
The suffering is inevitable,
And the pain is indelible.

www.ingramcontent.com/pod-product-compliance
Ingram Content Group UK Ltd.
Pitfield, Milton Keynes, MK11 3LW, UK
UKHW042000190726
13854UKWH00005B/2080

9 789353 478308